Collins

easy learning

Times tables workbook

Ages 5–7

Simon Greaves

How to use this book

- Easy Learning workbooks help your child improve basic skills, build confidence and develop a love of learning.
- Find a quiet, comfortable place to work, away from distractions.
- Get into a routine of completing one or two workbook pages with your child every day.
- Ask your child to circle the star that matches how many questions they have completed every two pages:

Some = half of the questions   Most = more than half   All = all the questions

- The progress certificate at the back of this book will help you and your child keep track of how many ★ have been circled.
- Encourage your child to work through all of the questions eventually, and praise them for completing the progress certificate.

- The ability to recall and use times tables facts is an essential skill and is invaluable for many mathematical processes.
- Learning tables at an early age gives your child confidence with numbers.

Parent tip
Look out for tips on how to help your child learn tables.

- Ask your child to find, count and colour in the little monkeys that are hidden throughout this book.
- This will help engage them with the pages of the book and get them interested in the activities.

(Don't count this one.)

The author and publisher are grateful to the copyright holders for permission to use quoted materials and images.

Cover: © Svetlana Ivanova / shutterstock.com & © lineartestpilot / shutterstock.com
p5, 6, 9, 16, 18, 20: © Asaf Eliason/ shutterstock.com

Published by Collins
An imprint of HarperCollinsPublishers
1 London Bridge Street
London SE1 9GF

Browse the complete Collins catalogue at www.collins.co.uk

First published in 2011
© HarperCollinsPublishers 2011
This edition © HarperCollinsPublishers 2015

10 9

ISBN-13 978-0-00-813439-6

The author asserts the moral right to be identified as the author of this work.

British Library Cataloguing in Publication Data

A Catalogue record for this publication is available from the British Library

Written by Simon Greaves
Design and layout by Linda Miles, Lodestone Publishing and Jouve
Illustrated by Graham Smith and Jenny Tulip
Cover design Sarah Duxbury and Paul Oates
Packaged and project managed by White-Thomson Publishing Ltd and Sonia Dawkins

Printed in Great Britain by Martins the Printers

Contents

Two times table

1 Fill in the missing answers.

$3 \times 2 =$ ☐ $12 \times 2 =$ ☐ $5 \times 2 =$ ☐

$6 \times 2 =$ ☐ $10 \times 2 =$ ☐ $2 \times 2 =$ ☐

$4 \times 2 =$ ☐ $8 \times 2 =$ ☐ $9 \times 2 =$ ☐

2 Colour yellow all the shapes that have an answer in the two times table.
What do you see?

_____

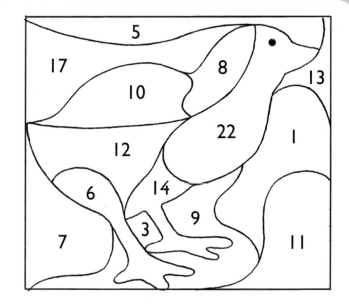

Parent tip
Sing the two times table along to the tune of a favourite song.

3 Here is a machine that multiplies numbers by two.
Fill in the missing numbers.

4 Count the coins and complete each multiplication.

3 × 2p = 6p	× 2p =	

---

5 Some of these football shirts have answers in the two times table.
Colour red all of the shirts that have an answer in the two times table.
Colour blue all of the shirts that do not.

 16   8   7   10   13   14   2

---

6 Colour a path through the number grid. You must only go through answers that are in the two times table.

21	3	23	7	18	→ Finish
5	7	9	10	14	
1	11	13	6	25	
19	8	20	22	3	
16	4	5	17	27	
2	1	13	15	29	

Start →

How much did you do?   Questions 1–6

Circle the star to show what you have done.

 Some   Most   All

Ten times table

The ten times table tells you how to count in sets of ten.

1 Fill in the missing answers.

$3 \times 10 =$ ☐ $6 \times 10 =$ ☐ $5 \times 10 =$ ☐

$9 \times 10 =$ ☐ $7 \times 10 =$ ☐ $8 \times 10 =$ ☐

$10 \times 10 =$ ☐ $2 \times 10 =$ ☐ $11 \times 10 =$ ☐

2 Find the total in each money box.

$3 \times 10p =$

$8 \times \quad p =$

$\quad \times \quad p =$

3 Count on or back in tens. Fill in the missing numbers in each row.

10	☐	30	☐	☐	☐	☐
100	☐	☐	70	☐	☐	☐
40	☐	☐	☐	☐	90	☐
120	☐	100	☐	☐	☐	

Parent tip
Chant the answers to the ten times table forwards and backwards.

4 Circle the numbers that are answers in the ten times table.

38   70   25   50   100   40   88   120   45   20

5 Complete these multiplications.

4 × 10 = ☐   9 × ☐ = 90

☐ × 10 = 70   10 × ☐ = 100

6 × ☐ = 60   ☐ × 10 = 30

5 × 10 = ☐   2 × 10 = ☐

☐ × 10 = 10   ☐ × 10 = 80

Parent tip
Look for answers in the ten times table on everyday objects.

6 Here are some objects on a shelf.
Find the number on each object then complete the multiplication.

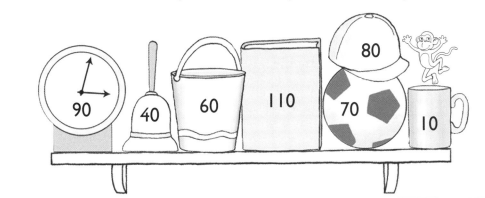

cap   ☐ = ☐ × 10   mug   ☐ = ☐ × 10

bucket   ☐ = ☐ × 10   book   ☐ = ☐ × 10

football ☐ = ☐ × 10   clock   ☐ = ☐ × 10

bell   ☐ = ☐ × 10

How much did you do?   Questions 1–6

Circle the star
to show what
you have done.

 Some   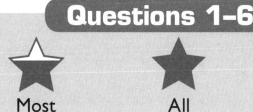 Most   All

Five times table

The five times table tells you how to count in sets of five.

1 Fill in the missing answers.

$3 \times 5 = \boxed{}$ $10 \times 5 = \boxed{}$ $5 \times 5 = \boxed{}$

$6 \times 5 = \boxed{}$ $7 \times 5 = \boxed{}$ $9 \times 5 = \boxed{}$

$12 \times 5 = \boxed{}$ $8 \times 5 = \boxed{}$ $2 \times 5 = \boxed{}$

2 Draw lines to join each key to the correct door.

45

15

35

25

50

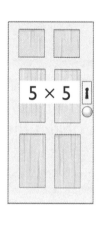

10×5 5×5 7×5

3×5 9×5

3 Here are some multiplications. Some are correct and some are not.
Put a tick next to those with the correct answer. ✔
Put a cross next to those with the wrong answer. ✘

$3 \times 5 = 15 \boxed{}$ $11 \times 5 = 55 \boxed{}$ $6 \times 5 = 25 \boxed{}$

$9 \times 5 = 45 \boxed{}$ $2 \times 5 = 10 \boxed{}$ $1 \times 5 = 10 \boxed{}$

$10 \times 5 = 45 \boxed{}$ $4 \times 5 = 25 \boxed{}$ $7 \times 5 = 35 \boxed{}$

4 In each line, circle the multiplication that matches the number in the box.

20	3 × 5	4 × 5	6 × 5	2 × 5
35	7 × 5	3 × 5	2 × 5	11 × 5
15	4 × 5	7 × 5	3 × 5	5 × 5
40	10 × 5	7 × 5	9 × 5	8 × 5

5 Draw coins to show the amount in each money box.

25p

15p

40p

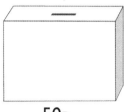
50p

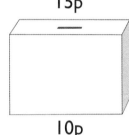
10p

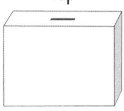
35p

6 The ship needs to reach the harbour. It must follow a route that only has answers to the five times table. Colour the route the ship must take.

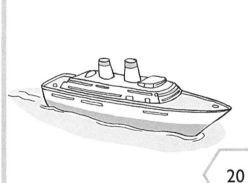

16
25   Finish
43
50   60
5   10
2   21
30   32
20   8   17
Start
46   3

Parent tip
Take turns with your child to recite alternate facts for the five times table.

How much did you do?   Questions 1–6

Circle the star
to show what
you have done.

Some

Most

All

Four times table

1 Fill in the missing answers.

$5 \times 4 = \boxed{}$ $\qquad$ $9 \times 4 = \boxed{}$ $\qquad$ $11 \times 4 = \boxed{}$

$4 \times 4 = \boxed{}$ $\qquad$ $2 \times 4 = \boxed{}$ $\qquad$ $10 \times 4 = \boxed{}$

$8 \times 4 = \boxed{}$ $\qquad$ $3 \times 4 = \boxed{}$ $\qquad$ $6 \times 4 = \boxed{}$

2 Choose the correct answer for each multiplication. Shade the letter next to that answer. The letters you have **not** shaded spell out a colour. What is the colour?

$3 \times 4 =$	12	s	or	15	P
$8 \times 4 =$	30	u	or	32	i
$5 \times 4 =$	20	l	or	22	r
$4 \times 4 =$	8	P	or	16	b
$9 \times 4 =$	30	l	or	36	a
$2 \times 4 =$	8	t	or	12	e

Parent tip
Ask your child to make a poster of the four times table to stick on the wall.

The colour is

3 Colour a path through the number grid. You must only go through numbers that are answers in the four times table.

21	33	38	22	40	8	→ Finish
2	31	44	24	36	13	
5	19	4	7	11	23	
1	9	32	18	14	3	
16	12	28	25	19	35	

Start →

4 Here is a machine that multiplies numbers by four.
Fill in the missing numbers.

3 →
8 →
4 →
9 →

× 4

→
→
→
→

Parent tip
Time how quickly your child can say the four times table.

5 Colour each square that is an answer in the four times table. Spot the pattern.

1	2	3	4	5	6	7	8	9	10
11	12	13	14	15	16	17	18	19	20
21	22	23	24	25	26	27	28	29	30
31	32	33	34	35	36	37	38	39	40
41	42	43	44	45	46	47	48	49	50

6 Colour in each circle that is an answer in the four times table.
What number can you see?

Use this number to complete the multiplication.

4 × ☐ = ☐

3   26   7   20
23   4   36   33   13
      1   38
24   40   8
11   17
16   28   37   32
21   10
40   12   4

Three times table

The three times table tells you how to count in sets of three.

1 Fill in the missing answers.

$3 \times 3 =$ ☐ $2 \times 3 =$ ☐ $6 \times 3 =$ ☐

$5 \times 3 =$ ☐ $8 \times 3 =$ ☐ $4 \times 3 =$ ☐

$10 \times 3 =$ ☐ $11 \times 3 =$ ☐ $7 \times 3 =$ ☐

2 Work out the answer to each multiplication on the parrot.
Use the answers to find the colours on the code key.
Colour the picture.

Code key
6 = green
12 = orange
21 = yellow
27 = light blue
30 = brown
36 = dark blue

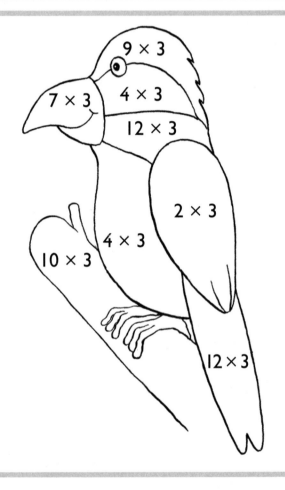

Parent tip
Record yourself saying the three times table for your child to listen to and repeat.

3 A balloon costs 3p.
How much will it cost to buy the following balloons?

5 balloons ☐ p   6 balloons ☐ p

9 balloons ☐ p   2 balloons ☐ p

4 balloons ☐ p   7 balloons ☐ p

3p

4 Look at the numbers in this machine.
Sort the numbers into those that are answers in the three times table and those that are not.

6   29   22
14   18
36
12   23   27
7   9   15

numbers in the **3** times table   numbers **not** in the 3 times table

5 Answer these questions.

What are eight threes? ⬜   What is 6 multiplied by 3? ⬜

Multiply 4 by 3. ⬜   Multiply seven by three. ⬜

What is nine multiplied by three? ⬜

What are the first six answers to the three times table?

⬜ ⬜ ⬜ ⬜ ⬜ ⬜

6 Complete these multiplications using the three times table.

⬜ × 3 = 15   ⬜ × 3 = 27   ⬜ × 3 = 9   ⬜ × 3 = 33

⬜ × 3 = 18   ⬜ × 3 = 3   ⬜ × 3 = 21   ⬜ × 3 = 6

How much did you do?   ## Questions 1–6

Circle the star to show what you have done.

Some

Most

All

Mixed tables

1 Fill in the missing answers.

$2 \times 2 =$ ☐ $7 \times 2 =$ ☐ $6 \times 2 =$ ☐ $1 \times 10 =$ ☐

$3 \times 10 =$ ☐ $9 \times 2 =$ ☐ $10 \times 10 =$ ☐ $11 \times 2 =$ ☐

$6 \times 10 =$ ☐ $3 \times 2 =$ ☐ $5 \times 10 =$ ☐ $2 \times 10 =$ ☐

$1 \times 2 =$ ☐ $4 \times 2 =$ ☐ $5 \times 2 =$ ☐ $7 \times 10 =$ ☐

$10 \times 2 =$ ☐ $8 \times 10 =$ ☐ $4 \times 10 =$ ☐ $9 \times 10 =$ ☐

2 Complete the multiplication grid.

×	3	6	9	10	7	12
2						
10						

Parent tip
Remember to ask your child to find and colour the monkey.

3 Work out the answer to each multiplication on the clown's face. Use the answers to find the correct colour in the code key. Colour the picture.

Code key
8 = pink
10 = yellow
14 = blue
18 = green
20 = red
40 = purple

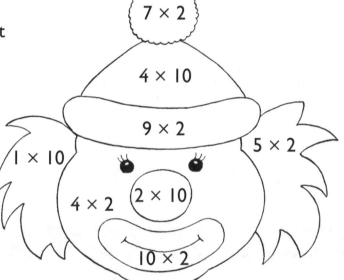

Parent tip
Record yourself saying the ten times table for your child to listen to and repeat.

14

4 Here are the prices of two items in a shop. How much will it cost to buy the following items?

6 pencils ☐ p   3 notebooks ☐ p

4 pencils ☐ p   5 notebooks ☐ p

8 pencils ☐ p   7 notebooks ☐ p

5 Write a multiplication to show the number of gloves in each group. Write another multiplication to show the number of fingers on the gloves in each group.

2 × 2 = 4   gloves
2 × 10 = 20   fingers

☐ × 2 = ☐   gloves
☐ × 10 = ☐   fingers

☐ × 2 = ☐   gloves
☐ × 10 = ☐   fingers

☐ × 2 = ☐   gloves
☐ × 10 = ☐   fingers

6 Count on or back in twos or tens. Fill in the missing numbers in each row.

2	☐	☐	8	☐	☐	☐
110	☐	90	☐	☐	☐	☐
20	☐	16	☐	☐	☐	☐
40	☐	☐	70	☐	☐	☐

15

Mixed tables

1 Write in the missing answers.

2 × 5 = ☐   8 × 10 = ☐   1 × 5 = ☐   8 × 5 = ☐

1 × 10 = ☐   11 × 5 = ☐   7 × 10 = ☐   4 × 10 = ☐

3 × 10 = ☐   6 × 10 = ☐   10 × 5 = ☐   9 × 5 = ☐

3 × 5 = ☐   10 × 10 = ☐   12 × 10 = ☐   5 × 5 = ☐

5 × 10 = ☐   4 × 5 = ☐   6 × 5 = ☐   9 × 10 = ☐

2 Colour red all the shapes that have an answer in the five or ten times tables. What do you see?

_____

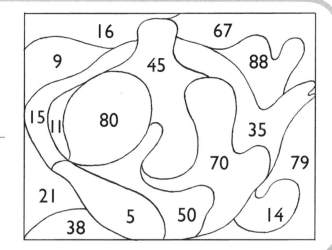

3 Work out the total amount of money in each purse.

☐ × 5p = ☐ p   ☐ × ☐ p = ☐ p   ☐ × ☐ p = ☐ p

☐ × ☐ p = ☐ p   ☐ × ☐ p = ☐ p

Complete the multiplication grid.

×	2	5	7	10	8	11
5						
10						

5 Fill in the missing numbers on each row by counting on or back in fives or tens.

5 10 ☐ ☐ ☐ 30 ☐

15 ☐ 25 ☐ ☐ 40 ☐

45 ☐ ☐ ☐ ☐ 20 ☐

70 ☐ ☐ ☐ 30 ☐ ☐

10 ☐ ☐ 40 ☐ ☐ ☐

Parent tip
Make flash cards of the five and ten times tables to test your child.

6 Try to answer all these questions in less than two minutes. Time yourself!

5 × 5 = ☐

35 = ☐ × ☐

1 × 10 = ☐

6 × 5 = ☐

100 = ☐ × ☐

4 × 5 = ☐

5 = ☐ × ☐

50 = ☐ × ☐

7 × 10 = ☐

25 = ☐ × ☐

How much did you do?   Questions 1–6

Circle the star to show what you have done.

Some

Most

All

Mixed tables

1 Fill in the answers to these multiplications.

3 × 2 = ☐   3 × 5 = ☐   1 × 2 = ☐

5 × 5 = ☐   1 × 5 = ☐   10 × 5 = ☐

4 × 5 = ☐   5 × 2 = ☐   7 × 5 = ☐

8 × 2 = ☐   7 × 2 = ☐   2 × 5 = ☐

4 × 2 = ☐   12 × 5 = ☐   9 × 2 = ☐

6 × 2 = ☐   9 × 5 = ☐   2 × 2 = ☐

6 × 5 = ☐   8 × 5 = ☐   2 × 10 = ☐

2 Write a multiplication to show the total amount of money in each of the groups below.

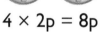

4 × 2p = 8p

☐ × 2p = ☐ p

☐ × 5p = ☐ p

☐ × ☐ p = ☐ p

☐ × ☐ p = ☐ p

3 Colour the fish that have answers in the two or five times tables.

50   22   11   23   12   35   18   7   45

4 Here are some targets. The arrow scores **five** times the number it lands on.
Work out the score for each target.

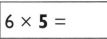 $6 \times 5 =$

The arrow scores **two** times the number it lands on.
Work out the score for each target.

 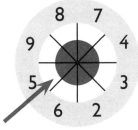 

$7 \times 2 =$

5 Draw a line to match each cup to the correct saucer.

| 1×2 | 5×5 | 3×2 | 2×5 | 8×2 |

| 6 | 10 | 16 | 2 | 25 |

6 Complete these multiplications using the two and five times tables.

$\square \times 5 = 25$ $\square \times 2 = 18$ $\square \times 2 = 24$ $\square \times 2 = 8$

$\square \times 5 = 20$ $\square \times 5 = 60$ $\square \times 2 = 10$

$\square \times 5 = 40$ $\square \times 2 = 12$ $\square \times 5 = 50$

How much did you do? **Questions 1–6**

Circle the star to show what you have done.

 Some   Most  All

Mixed tables

1 Write in the missing answers.

$3 \times 10 = \boxed{}$ $8 \times 2 = \boxed{}$ $4 \times 10 = \boxed{}$ $5 \times 2 = \boxed{}$

$7 \times 5 = \boxed{}$ $3 \times 5 = \boxed{}$ $5 \times 5 = \boxed{}$ $10 \times 10 = \boxed{}$

$6 \times 2 = \boxed{}$ $12 \times 10 = \boxed{}$ $3 \times 2 = \boxed{}$ $6 \times 10 = \boxed{}$

$4 \times 5 = \boxed{}$ $9 \times 2 = \boxed{}$ $6 \times 5 = \boxed{}$ $10 \times 5 = \boxed{}$

2 Work out the total amount of money in each purse.

$\boxed{} \times 2p = \boxed{}$ p

$\boxed{} \times 5p = \boxed{}$ p

$\boxed{} \times 10p = \boxed{}$ p

$\boxed{} \times \boxed{} p = \boxed{}$ p

$\boxed{} \times \boxed{} p = \boxed{}$ p

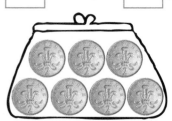

$\boxed{} \times \boxed{} p = \boxed{}$ p

3 Complete the multiplication grid.

×	2	5	8	1	9	11
2						
10						
5						

Parent tip
Find totals for piles of the same coin using 2p, 5p and 10p coins.

4 Write the missing numbers on each machine.

5 Here are the prices of some vegetables in a shop.
How much will it cost to buy the following vegetables?

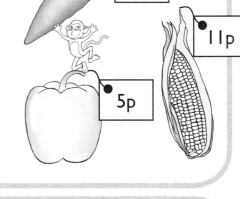

8 corncobs ☐ p   9 peppers ☐ p

10 carrots ☐ p   7 peppers ☐ p

5 carrots ☐ p   3 corncobs ☐ p

How many peppers can you buy for 30p? ☐

6 Work out the missing number to complete the multiplication on each safe.
Find this number in the boxes below the safes. Write the letter from that safe in the box. What is the hidden word?

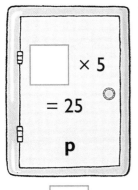 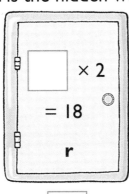 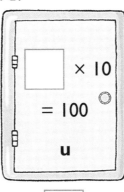 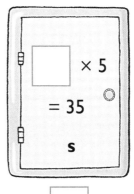 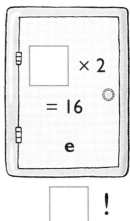

☐ ☐ ☐ ☐ ☐ !

7   10   5   8   9

Mixed tables

Threes and fours

1 Fill in the missing answers.

4 × 3 = ☐	9 × 4 = ☐	7 × 3 = ☐	10 × 3 = ☐
5 × 4 = ☐	1 × 4 = ☐	10 × 4 = ☐	8 × 3 = ☐
1 × 3 = ☐	6 × 4 = ☐	6 × 3 = ☐	7 × 4 = ☐
8 × 4 = ☐	3 × 3 = ☐	11 × 4 = ☐	4 × 4 = ☐
9 × 3 = ☐	2 × 3 = ☐	3 × 4 = ☐	12 × 3 = ☐

2 Draw a line to match each butterfly to the correct flower.

3 × 3   8 × 3   6 × 3   5 × 3
12 × 4   4 × 4   8 × 4   10 × 4

18   40   32   48   9   16   15   24

3 Here are some multiplications. Some are correct and some are not.
Put a tick next to those with the correct answer. ✔
Put a cross next to those with the wrong answer. ✗

2 × 3 = 7 ☐	5 × 3 = 15 ☐	11 × 4 = 44 ☐
6 × 4 = 24 ☐	7 × 4 = 32 ☐	9 × 3 = 30 ☐
8 × 3 = 24 ☐	2 × 4 = 8 ☐	4 × 3 = 14 ☐

4 A spade costs 3p. A bucket costs 4p.
How much will it cost to buy the following items?

6 spades ☐ p   3 buckets ☐ p

4 spades ☐ p   5 buckets ☐ p

8 spades ☐ p   7 buckets ☐ p

☐

How many spades can you buy with 15p? ☐

5 Complete the multiplication fact that describes each pattern.

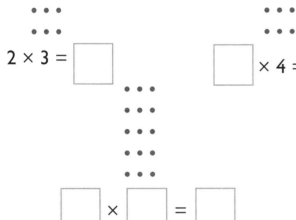

$2 \times 3 =$ ☐

☐ $\times 4 =$ ☐

☐ $\times 4 =$ ☐

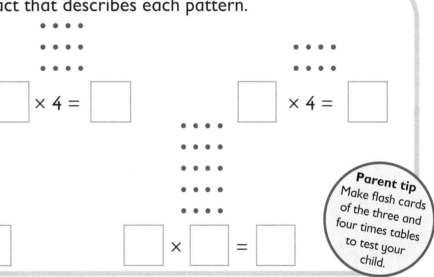

☐ $\times$ ☐ $=$ ☐

☐ $\times$ ☐ $=$ ☐

Parent tip
Make flash cards of the three and four times tables to test your child.

6 The bird needs to get to the nest.
Colour in the trees to make a path for the bird.
You must only colour trees that are answers in the three or four times tables.

How much did you do?   **Questions 1–6**

Circle the star
to show what
you have done.

Some   Most   All

Mixed tables

1 Fill in the missing answers.

4 × 2 = ☐   2 × 4 = ☐   4 × 4 = ☐   3 × 2 = ☐

6 × 2 = ☐   11 × 4 = ☐   1 × 4 = ☐   10 × 4 = ☐

7 × 2 = ☐   8 × 2 = ☐   5 × 2 = ☐   10 × 2 = ☐

5 × 4 = ☐   6 × 4 = ☐   7 × 4 = ☐   8 × 4 = ☐

1 × 2 = ☐   9 × 4 = ☐   9 × 2 = ☐   2 × 2 = ☐

2 Here are the prices of two items in a shop.
How much will it cost to buy the following items?

6 yo-yos ☐ p 11 balls ☐ p

10 yo-yos ☐ p   3 balls ☐ p

8 balls ☐ p   12 yo-yos ☐ p

How many yo-yos can you buy for 10p? ☐

3 Colour each shape that is an answer in the two or four times table.
What do you see? _____

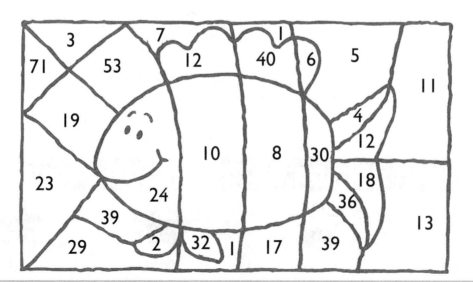

24

4 Complete the multiplication grid.

×	4	7	9	10	3	12
4						
2						

5 Complete the times tables wheels for the two and four times tables.

6 Look at the answer on each calculator.
Write the multiplication by two or four that gives that answer.

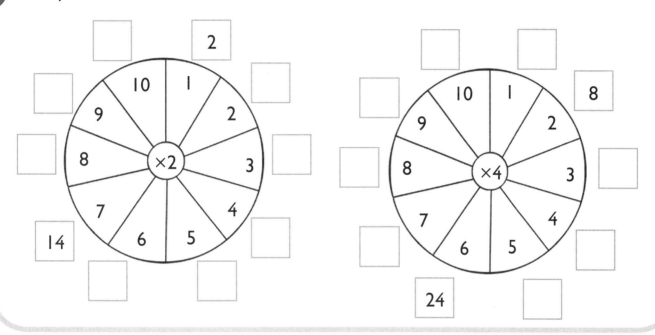

☐ × ☐ = 18

☐ × 2 = ☐

☐ × 4 = ☐

☐ × 2 = ☐

☐ × 4 = ☐

Mixed tables

1 Fill in the missing answers.

3 × 3 = ☐   9 × 5 = ☐   6 × 5 = ☐   8 × 3 = ☐

6 × 3 = ☐   2 × 5 = ☐   5 × 3 = ☐   5 × 5 = ☐

1 × 3 = ☐   3 × 5 = ☐   11 × 5 = ☐   10 × 3 = ☐

9 × 3 = ☐   10 × 5 = ☐   4 × 3 = ☐   8 × 5 = ☐

7 × 3 = ☐   2 × 3 = ☐   7 × 5 = ☐   1 × 5 = ☐

2 Here are some items for sale in a shop.
How much will it cost to buy the following items?

3 spoons ☐ p   8 spoons ☐ p

7 forks ☐ p   5 knives ☐ p

4 spoons ☐ p   6 forks ☐ p

How many knives can you buy with 15p? ☐

How many spoons can you buy with 15p? ☐

5p

5p

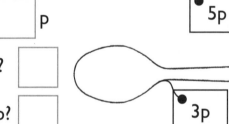
3p

3 Colour a path through the number grid. You must only go through answers that are in the three or five times tables.

23	13	4	29	31	27	→ Finish
11	41	2	30	21	50	
8	22	9	36	37	32	
1	29	3	7	19	28	
10	18	45	17	26	44	

Start →

4 Here are some targets.
If an arrow lands in the white ring it scores 3 times the number it lands on.
If an arrow lands in the blue ring it scores 5 times the number it lands on.
Complete the score for each target.

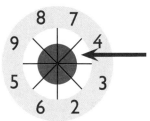

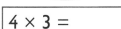

$4 \times 3 =$

$9 \times 5 =$

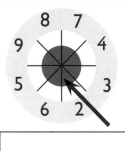

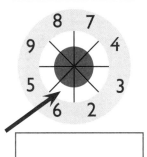

5 In each line, circle the multiplication or multiplications that match the number in the triangle.

 18   1×3 4×3 6×3 9×3

40   5×5 7×5 6×5 8×5

30   9×5 10×3 11×3 9×3

 15   5×5 3×5 8×5 5×3

6 Count on in threes and fives to complete the scarves.

Which two numbers appear on both scarves?

[   ] and [   ]

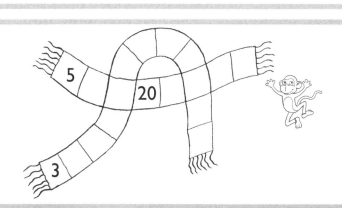

Mixed tables

Twos, threes, fours, fives and tens

1 Complete these multiplications.

30 = ☐ × 5   24 = ☐ × 4   90 = ☐ × 10

18 = ☐ × 2   45 = ☐ × 5   12 = ☐ × 3

32 = ☐ × 4   21 = ☐ × 3   16 = ☐ × 4

20 = ☐ × 2 or ☐ × 4 or ☐ × 5 or ☐ × 10

2 Here are the prices of some pieces of fruit in a shop.

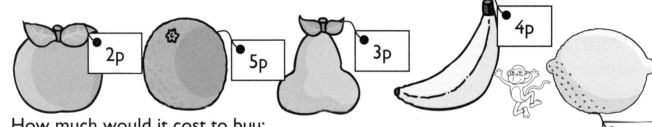

2p   5p   3p   4p

10p

How much would it cost to buy:

5 oranges ☐ p   11 apples ☐ p   3 bananas ☐ p

9 pears ☐ p   6 lemons ☐ p

How many pears can you buy with 36p? ☐

3 Start from 3 and count on in threes up to 30, joining the black dots as you go. Then start from 4 and count on in fours up to 40, joining the blue dots.

What do you see?

_____

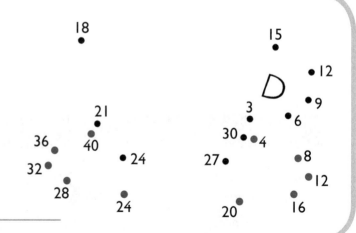

4 Choose a number card from the top row and a multiplication card from the bottom row.
Write out and complete your multiplication in the box.
Find at least ten multiplications.

| 4 | 6 | 3 | 12 | 9 |

| × 5 | × 2 | × 4 | × 3 | ×10 |

5 Draw lines to join the multiplications that have the same answers.

| 5 × 4 | 3 × 4 | 6 × 4 | 10 × 3 | 9 × 2 |

(6 × 5)　(2 × 10)　(6 × 3)　(6 × 2)　(8 × 3)

6 Find the missing numbers in the pyramids.
Multiply the two numbers next to each other to work out the number in the block above.

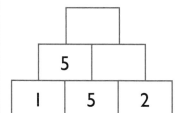

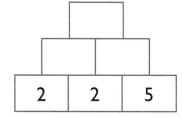

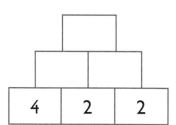

Answers

Two times table

Page 4

1 6, 24, 10, 12, 20, 4, 8, 16, 18
2 Colour 22, 6, 8, 10, 12, 14. It's a bird!
3 8, 14, 18, 24

Page 5

4 $7 \times 2p = 14p$; $5 \times 2p = 10p$; $9 \times 2p = 18p$; $6 \times 2p = 12p$
5 Colour red 16, 8, 10, 14, 2; colour blue 7, 13
6 Colour 2, 16, 4, 8, 20, 22, 6, 10, 14, 18

Ten times table

Page 6

1 30, 60, 50, 90, 70, 80, 100, 20, 110
2 $3 \times 10p = 30p$; $8 \times 10p = 80p$; $9 \times 10p = 90p$; $5 \times 10p = 50p$
3 20, 40, 50, 60, 70; 90, 80, 60, 50, 40; 50, 60, 70, 80, 100; 110, 90, 80, 70, 60

Page 7

4 Circle 70, 50, 100, 40, 120, 20
5 40, 10, 7, 10, 10, 3, 50, 20, 1, 8
6 Cap $80 = 8 \times 10$; bucket $60 = 6 \times 10$; football $70 = 7 \times 10$; bell $40 = 4 \times 10$; mug $10 = 1 \times 10$; book $110 = 11 \times 10$; clock $90 = 9 \times 10$

Five times table

Page 8

1 15, 50, 25, 30, 35, 45, 60, 40, 10
2 45 and 9×5; 15 and 3×5; 35 and 7×5; 25 and 5×5; 50 and 10×5
3 ✔, ✔, ✗, ✔, ✔, ✗, ✗, ✗, ✔

Page 9

4 Circle 4×5, 7×5, 3×5, 8×5
5 3 coins, 8 coins, 10 coins, 2 coins, 7 coins
6 Colour 20, 30, 5, 50, 10, 60, 25

Four times table

Page 10

1 20, 36, 44, 16, 8, 40, 32, 12, 24
2 Purple
3 Start, 16, 12, 28, 32, 4, 44, 24, 36, 40, 8, Finish

Page 11

4 12, 32, 16, 36
5 Colour 4, 8, 12, 16, 20, 24, 28, 32, 36, 40, 44, 48
6 Colour 4, 24, 16, 40 and 20, 36, 40, 28, 12, 4, 32, 8; 16; $4 \times 4 = 16$

Three times tables

Page 12

1 9, 6, 18, 15, 24, 12, 30, 33, 21
2 7×3 = yellow; 9×3 = light blue; 4×3 = orange; 12×3 = dark blue; 2×3 = green; 10×3 = brown
3 15p, 18p, 27p, 6p, 12p, 21p

Page 13

4 Numbers in the three times table – 6, 18, 12, 15, 27, 9 , 36; not in the three times table –   29, 22, 14, 23, 7
5 24; 18; 12; 21; 27; 3, 6, 9, 12, 15, 18
6 5, 9, 3, 11, 6, 1, 7, 2

Mixed tables (twos and tens)

Page 14

1 4, 14, 12, 10, 30, 18, 100, 22, 60, 6, 50, 20, 2, 8, 10, 70, 20, 80, 40, 90
2 $\times 2$ – 6, 12, 18, 20, 14, 24; $\times 10$ – 30, 60, 90, 100, 70, 120
3 4×2 = pink; 1×10 and 5×2 = yellow; 7×2 = blue; 9×2 = green; 2×10 and 10×2 = red; 4×10 = purple

Page 15

4 12p, 30p, 8p, 50p, 16p, 70p
5 $6 \times 2 = 12$, $6 \times 10 = 60$; $5 \times 2 = 10$, $5 \times 10 = 50$; $3 \times 2 = 6$, $3 \times 10 = 30$
6 4, 6, 10, 12, 14; 100, 80, 70, 60, 50; 18, 14, 12, 10, 8; 50, 60, 80, 90, 100

Mixed tables (fives and tens)

Page 16

1 10, 80, 5, 40, 10, 55, 70, 40, 30, 60, 50, 45, 15, 100, 120, 25, 50, 20, 30, 90
2 Colour 5, 15, 35, 45, 50, 70, 80. It's a teapot!
3 $6 \times 5p = 30p$; $5 \times 5p = 25p$; $4 \times 10p = 40p$; $2 \times 10p = 20p$; $9 \times 5p = 45p$

Page 17

4 ×5 – 10, 25, 35, 50, 40, 55; ×10 – 20, 50, 70, 100, 80, 110

5 15, 20, 25, 35; 20, 30, 35, 45; 40, 35, 30, 25, 15; 60, 50, 40, 20, 10; 20, 30, 50, 60, 70

6 25, 20, 7 × 5, 1 × 5, 10, 10 × 5 or 5 × 10, 30, 70, 10 × 10, 5 × 5

Mixed tables (twos and fives)

Page 18

1 6, 15, 2, 25, 5, 50, 20, 10, 35, 16, 14, 10, 8, 60, 18, 12, 45, 4, 30, 40, 20

2 6 × 2p = 12p; 6 × 5p = 30p; 3 × 5p = 15p; 3 × 2p = 6p

3 Colour 22, 50, 35, 18, 12, 45

Page 19

4 6 × 5 = 30, 8 × 5 = 40, 4 × 5 = 20; 7 × 2 = 14, 5 × 2 = 10, 9 × 2 = 18

5 1 × 2 and 2; 5 × 5 and 25; 3 × 2 and 6; 2 × 5 and 10; 8 × 2 and 16

6 5, 9, 12, 4, 4, 12, 5, 8, 6, 10

Mixed tables (twos, fives and tens)

Page 20

1 30, 16, 40, 10, 35, 15, 25, 100, 12, 120, 6, 60, 20, 18, 30, 50

2 6 × 2p = 12p; 9 × 5p = 45p; 5 × 10p = 50p; 6 × 5p = 30p; 7 × 10p = 70p; 7 × 2p = 14p

3 ×2 – 4, 10, 16, 2, 18, 22; ×10 – 20, 50, 80, 10, 90, 110; ×5 – 10, 25, 40, 5, 45, 55

Page 21

4 10, 60, 25, 7; 10, 30, 60, 9

5 88p, 45p, 20p, 35p, 10p, 33p; 6 peppers

6 5, 9, 10, 7, 8; super!

Mixed tables (threes and fours)

Page 22

1 12, 36, 21, 30, 20, 4, 40, 24, 3, 24, 18, 28, 32, 9, 44, 16, 27, 6, 12, 36

2 3 × 3 and 9; 12 × 4 and 48; 8 × 3 and 24; 4 × 4 and 16; 6 × 3 and 18; 8 × 4 and 32; 5 × 3 and 15: 10 × 4 and 40

3 ✗, ✔, ✔, ✔, ✗, ✗, ✔, ✔, ✗

Page 23

4 18p, 12p, 12p, 20p, 24p, 28p, 5 spades

5 2 × 3 = 6; 3 × 4 = 12; 2 × 4 = 8; 5 × 3 = 15; 5 × 4 = 20

6 Colour 6, 16, 21, 30, 4, 8, 24, 27, 36, 28

Mixed tables (twos and fours)

Page 24

1 8, 8, 16, 6, 12, 44, 4, 40, 14, 16, 10, 20, 20, 24, 28, 32, 2, 36, 18, 4

2 12p, 44p, 20p, 12p, 32p, 24p, 5 yo-yos

3 Colour 12, 40, 6, 24, 10, 8, 30, 4, 12, 18, 36, 2, 32; it's a fish!

Page 25

4 ×4 – 16, 28, 36, 40, 12, 48; ×2 – 8, 14, 18, 20, 6, 24

5 4, 6, 8, 10, 12, 16, 18, 20; 4, 12, 16, 20, 28, 32, 36, 40

6 9 × 2 = 18; 8 × 2 = 16; 4 × 4 = 16; 10 × 2 = 20; 5 × 4 = 20

Mixed tables (threes and fives)

Page 26

1 9, 45, 30, 24, 18, 10, 15, 25, 3, 15, 55, 30, 27, 50, 12, 40, 21, 6, 35, 5

2 9p, 24p, 35p, 25p, 12p, 30p, 3 knives, 5 spoons

3 10, 18, 45, 3, 9, 36, 30, 21, 50, 27

Page 27

4 12, 45, 7 × 3 = 21; 2 × 5 = 10; 6 × 3 = 18; 4 × 5 = 20

5 6 × 3; 8 × 5; 10 × 3; 3 × 5 and 5 × 3

6 10, 15, 25, 30, 35, 40; 6, 9, 12, 15, 18, 21, 24, 27, 30, 33, 36; 15 and 30

Mixed tables (twos, threes, fours, fives and tens)

Page 28

1 6, 6, 9, 9, 9, 4, 8, 7, 4; 10, 5, 4, 2

2 25p, 22p, 12p, 27p, 60p, 12 pears

3 Teacup and saucer

Page 29

4 There are 25 possible answers

5 5 × 4 and 2 × 10; 3 × 4 and 6 × 2; 6 × 4 and 8 × 3; 10 × 3 and 6 × 5; 9 × 2 and 6 × 3

6 Middle 10, top 50; middle 4 and 10, top 40; middle 8 and 4, top 32

Check your progress

- Shade in the stars on the progress certificate to show how much you did. Shade one star for every ⭐ you circled in this book.
- If you have shaded fewer than 10 stars go back to the pages where you circled Some ⭐ or Most ⭐ and try those pages again.
- If you have shaded 10 or more stars, well done!

Collins Easy Learning Times Tables Age 5–7 Workbook

Progress certificate

name _____

to

date _____

Two	Ten	Five	Four	Three	Twos and tens	Fives and tens	Twos and fives	Twos, fives and tens	Threes and fours	Twos and fours	Threes and fives	Twos, threes, fours, fives and tens
Pages 4 & 5	Pages 6 & 7	Pages 8 & 9	Pages 10 & 11	Pages 12 & 13	Pages 14 & 15	Pages 16 & 17	Pages 18 & 19	Pages 20 & 21	Pages 22 & 23	Pages 24 & 25	Pages 26 & 27	Pages 28 & 29
☆ 1	☆ 2	☆ 3	☆ 4	☆ 5	☆ 6	☆ 7	☆ 8	☆ 9	☆ 10	☆ 11	☆ 12	☆ 13